Thumbs Up for *Take Heart!*

"After years of success with matching up happy singles, Amy Owens deeply understands the difference between singles who are successful in finding love and those who aren't. The Ten Lessons in this book are as on-target as anything I've seen, and if the real-life stories she generously shares don't inspire and encourage you, you better check your pulse. You'll find useful ideas in this book, no matter how long you've been single. Amy goes to the heart of what you need to find love."

— Susan Page, author of *If I'm So Wonderful, Why Am I Still Single?*

"Every divorced or widowed person who is considering re-marriage should read *Take Heart!*"

— Rev. Jim Russell, Singles Pastor

"Using true-life stories to demonstrate their effectiveness, Amy Owens identifies ten principles designed to help singles feel confident in their dating relationships. Men and women will be encouraged as they *Take Heart!* and practice the skills suggested by The Singles Coach"

— Terri Coe, Director, St. Luke's Singles

"*Take Heart!* is easy to read; it literally flows. Most importantly, it contains practical, common sense advice supported by real-life stories. I believe it will change people's lives!"

— Frank Basile, Author, Columnist, Professional Speaker

Take Heart!

by Amy M. Owens, M.A.
The Singles Coach

Take Heart!

Stories of Encouragement for Singles

PLUS — Ten Lessons You'll Need
To Find Mr. or Ms. Right

Published by
Connections Publishing
9465 Counselors Row, Suite 200
Indianapolis, Indiana, 46240

Copyright 2002 by Amy M. Owens
All rights reserved.
Printed by **Western Newspaper Publishing Co.**
Printed in the United States of America

ISBN 0-9705301-0-2
Library of Congress Catalog Card Number: 00-110200

The stories in this book are true. However, in some cases, the names and/or circumstances have been slightly altered to protect the privacy of the people involved.

I dedicate this book to my beloved husband, Jim, whose devotion, love and support is the wind beneath my wings.

Special Thanks To –

Abby Marmion, my publicist and marketing guru, who encouraged me to write this book and provided the expertise I needed along the way.

Scott Barratt who dubbed me "The Singles Coach."

Joe Lawn who helped me design the "Advanced Relationship Strategies for Singles" course.

Dick Surber, whose question, "So, Amy, when are you going to write your book?" prompted me to give the idea serious consideration.

The members of **"The Artist's Way"** group ably led by **Amy Barnes** whose caring helped me identify, face and walk through the fears I had about this project.

Bill Brooks, my editor, who has encouraged my writing through the many years of our special friendship and taught me how very redundant the word "very" is!

Anne Walker, who supported me through my divorce, for graciously proofreading the initial manuscript.

Donna Cambra, the graphic designer whose creative touch made this book attractive and easy-to-read.

My sons and **extended family** for their interest, support and confidence in me.

The **10 couples** and other **students** who shared their personal stories so that others might benefit.

Contents

Introduction

When Life Gives You Lemons, Make Lemonade

In 1989, life dumped a ton of lemons on me — an unanticipated and unwelcome divorce after 24 years of marriage. Over the next several years, I dug my way out.

In 1995, I made a commitment to teach others how to do the same. Five years and hundreds of graduates later, I now have the opportunity to share stories from a few of those "others". You will read about 10 of the students who completed my course, "Advanced Relationship Strategies for Singles" (ARS) and successfully followed my lead.

These 10 students took to heart the lessons I shared with them and graduated from the course with the information and confidence they needed. Then, they went out and did the hard work of putting the lessons into practice.

I designed ARS to teach singles how to get themselves ready from the inside out to attract Mr. or Ms. Right into their lives. ARS is "the singles course" I refer to throughout this book.

In writing this book, I chose to couple true love stories with lessons. Stories warm the heart while allowing us to imagine ourselves doing (or not doing) what the people in the story did. Lessons provide us the guidance and information we need to change our thinking and to take action to change our lives.

After reading these stories, I hope you find yourself thinking, "If he or she can do it, so can I!"

By the way, I married my Mr. Right in 1999. How's that for turning lemons into lemonade?

Additional information about the ARS course is available
on my Web site: **www.thesinglescoach.com.**

Chapter 1

Katie and Carl – A Love Story

It was the first night of class, and I was looking forward to meeting my new students for the first time. When Katie came striding up the walk, I was struck by how beautiful she was. As is my custom, I extended my hand and introduced myself to her. Katie, however, barely acknowledged me. With her body turned slightly away from me, she did not make eye contact with me nor did she shake my hand. Somewhat startled, I asked if she was here for the singles class. She said, "Yes." When I asked her name, she said, "I'm Katie." Nothing more.

It wasn't until much later that her classmates and I learned what prompted Katie's behavior.

A tall, slender young woman with thick shoulder-length brunette hair and crystal blue eyes, Katie was 37 and had never married. She wanted more than anything else to be married.

Physically challenged by cerebral palsy as a result of birth trauma, Katie's right hand hung limply from her wrist. She typically carried her right arm across her waist with her hand tucked behind the other arm.

Katie's avoidant behavior was her way of putting the rest of us on notice that she didn't want her physical differentness acknowledged. In her mind, acknowledging it would make the difference "real" and would make her different from the rest of us.

It was painful for Katie to hear that her classmates and I were not willing to pretend we didn't notice her hand. It is a part of who she is. We liked Katie and wanted to get to know her more. Whenever she tried to hide her hand, she introduced an awkward element into social interactions. More importantly for us, in trying to hide her hand, she unwittingly hid her beautiful inner self from us, too.

We learned a lot from Katie about being physically disabled in a physically able world. And Katie learned that being perceived as approachable was more important in attracting people to her than creating a false image of her physical self.

What happened to Katie? Well, encouraged by her classmates, Katie began to attend singles dances with them. That's when we discovered what a beautiful dancer she is. "When all my girl friends were playing volleyball, I was taking ballroom dance lessons. I love to dance," she told us. At one of those dances, Katie met Carl, a handsome gray-haired man who, like Katie, is an accomplished dancer.

Katie and Carl hit it off from the beginning, talking easily with each other between dances. At the end of the evening, they exchanged phone numbers. They met the next day for lunch and spent 3 hours lost in conversation with each other. The following evening they went dancing together again. In class, Katie appeared more relaxed, confident and playful than we had seen her before. She told us about the fun she and Carl were having dancing and getting to know each other. As she talked, she used *both* arms to talk with, not just one.

Carl, a prince of a man, is a carpenter. As a result of an accident with a saw, Carl is missing the first knuckle on each of two fingers of his left hand. Katie's limp hand was not a problem for Carl. Ever the kidder, Carl reasoned that, "If she gets mad at me for something I've done, that's one less hand she has to smack me with!"

Carl was the first man that Katie allowed to see her as she really is — beautiful inside and out.

Katie and Carl married this year. Her classmates and I danced at their wedding, but the bride and groom stole the show. Katie and Carl — a real love story.

Lesson #1

Approachability and Self-Esteem are Required

To attract Mr. or Ms. Right, you must be approachable. If you aren't approachable, it doesn't matter who you are, what you've accomplished or how much money you make. People are attracted to other people who are approachable.

What exactly do I mean by "approachable"? Let me give you an example. Imagine that you are out somewhere, the grocery store perhaps, and don't have a watch. There are no clocks in sight, and you need to know what time it is. You have to ask somebody to tell you what time it is. You look around. There are several people near you. Which one of the several people do you ask?

Whomever you would choose has the quality of being approachable. That is, you would feel OK about initiating a contact. Something about them gives you the idea that you would likely get a positive response.

What goes into being approachable? Typically, the approachable person is someone who returns your eye contact with "soft eyes" or a friendly look. They may smile or make a friendly comment. They appear to be interested in what they are doing but not totally preoccupied with it. They don't seem to be in a big hurry. If they are with someone, like a child or a friend, they are treating them well and vice versa.

By the way, if in the example above you would have chosen not to ask for the time, you may be someone who would not be seen by others as approachable. That independent streak that makes it difficult for you to reach out for assistance may reflect an unwillingness or a fearfulness on your part to have others approach you or be close to you. I'm not saying this is necessarily so about you, but it's something to think about. Loving is about giving and receiving. To be loved, we have to be willing to be vulnerable enough to both give love and receive love.

To find out if you're approachable, ask your friends or people in your social circle. If it's OK with the person you ask, you might write down what they tell you. That way, you can refer to your notes and think about what they said to you later when you are alone. If you don't understand what they are telling you, ask them to say it a different way or to give you examples.

While someone is giving you feedback, it's a good idea to stifle your urge to justify or explain your behavior. If you justify or explain, you are likely to miss the point and lose the benefit of what they are saying to you. Just try to take in everything they say to you the way a reporter takes notes on everything that is said or happens in an interview and then later writes the story — after he or she has had the chance to digest what he/she heard.

Regardless of what your friends tell you, accept their feedback as a gift because that is what it is. It's usually pretty difficult for people to tell us what we need to know about ourselves but don't really want to hear. The people we ask are in a bind. They want to tell us the truth, and they also don't want to hurt our feelings. This may be especially difficult if they don't usually speak on such a frank level.

To increase your approachability, get some feedback from people you know and trust. Think about it and make changes accordingly.

A final note before we leave this topic. The most important thing you can do to be seen as approachable is to smile.

Smiling sends one or more of these messages: "I'm friendly." "I'm a nice person." "I'd like you to respond to me." "I would be OK if you approached me." If you are already a smiler, keep smiling. If you're not, please start smiling.

To help you develop the habit, make it a point to smile in your rearview mirror every time you have to wait at a stoplight. If the driver behind you is sitting on your bumper, smile and wave. He or she will back off after the light changes.

Remember Carl, the "prince of a man?" He's a very shy man who feels uncomfortable with people he doesn't know. When he's out in public, Carl doesn't talk much. He just listens and smiles. Everyone thinks Carl is the nicest man — which he is.

Self-esteem is also required in order to attract Mr. or Ms. Right. A lot has been written about self-esteem. Here are my thoughts on the subject.

Self-Esteem

Self-esteem is about being OK with yourself. It's viewing yourself as good enough. It means seeing yourself as measuring up, being worthwhile and fitting in as a human being.

When I was single, I included these affirmations in my morning prayers: "I am loved, I am loving, and I am lovable." The words "I am loved" reminded me that even though I was single and un-partnered, there were a number of people who loved me. "I am loving" prompted me to continue to treat others with loving kindness. The words "I am lovable" were a reminder that I was OK with myself.

If I am OK with myself first, then it is possible for me to be perceived as OK by others. First I love me, then others love me. By esteeming myself, I set up the possibility of others esteeming me. Being loved by others begins as an "inside job".

If I have low self-esteem, how do I raise it? If I have no self-esteem, how do I learn to esteem myself? Again, much has been written in this area, and I refer you to your local library or book-store to find books and strategies that appeal to you. Don't worry too much about finding the perfect program or "the best" pro-gram. There is no such thing. The only program worth following is the one that works for you, and the one that will work for you is likely the one you are naturally attracted to. Trust your instincts to pick the right one for yourself.

One time, when my self-esteem was at a low point, a mentor, Joe Cruse, gave me this to think about: "In all of time and in all of creation, you are the only you there ever was or ever will be. There never was before, and there will never be again another YOU." Jim Russell, a singles pastor in Michigan says, "You are an irrepeatable miracle of God." You are the original, and there are no carbon copies. You are truly unique, truly special. You are a one-of-a-kind combination of gifts, talents, preferences and quirks. You have strengths and weaknesses. Let's remember that every strength is a weakness and every weakness is a strength.

Self-esteem is feeling good on the inside about who we are. Esteeming ourselves means valuing the skills we have mastered as well as the inborn traits we have which make us unique. It's OK to esteem our intelligence, honesty, integrity, creativity, work ethic, patience and loyalty as well as our height, physical strength, hair type and eye color.

To raise our self-esteem, we need to let go of the discouraging idea that we have to be like everybody else to be acceptable, desirable or attractive to others. Because human beings are a universe of unique, one-of-a-kind individuals, then, by definition, we cannot be like everybody else. It is impossible to be like everyone else if every one is unique.

A realistic, healthy and encouraging view is to see ourselves as good enough. Not the greatest, not THE BEST, but simply good enough — worthwhile, worthy. Self-esteem is, after all, another term for self-worth.

Change Erroneous Beliefs

Katie thought she had to be totally self-sufficient and that she had to be exactly like everybody else. These beliefs kept her feeling worthy. And, as long as she felt unworthy, she unwittingly kept pushing love away, even though being loved is what she wanted most in the world. We human beings are amazing, aren't we?

The important thing here is not that Katie had mistaken beliefs — we all do — but that she was willing to change them. Once she did, she quickly got what she wanted. It doesn't always happen so quickly but it does happen. Believe it.

Does this discussion make you uncomfortable? Are you thinking that I am encouraging you to become prideful, arrogant or stuck on yourself in an unhealthy or unpleasant way? I'm not.

Pride vs. Self-Esteem

Pride and self-esteem are not the same thing. Pride is an "outside job" while self-esteem is an "inside" one. Pride is feeling good about what we have in the outer world such as the new car we just bought, the house we live in, or the amount of money we earn. Self-esteem is feeling good on the inside about who we are.

We feel proud when we accomplish something in the outer world, such as when we complete a degree, win a championship or earn a promotion. On the other hand, when we do the right thing, like overcoming a difficult challenge or struggling through a difficult time, we feel healthy self-esteem.

Taking pride in oneself is generally considered a positive trait as when we say that someone takes pride in his/her car or job. The difficulty lies in the fact that the good feeling is based on having the item in our possession. What happens when we no longer have it? Or, what happens if we have a lot of tangibles but little self-esteem?

The key to becoming a happy, emotionally healthy human is to have a little pride and a lot of self-esteem. Without self-esteem, our accomplishments and possessions mean nothing. High-pride people with low self-esteem often feel like impostors, and other people may, in fact, refer to them as phonies. When you feel like an imposter, the last thing you want is to be "found out." So you build walls of defense and try to keep other people from getting close enough to discover your secret. You sabotage relationships rather than reveal yourself.

When you have high self-esteem, you value yourself unconditionally. It doesn't matter if you are enjoying a time of feasting or experiencing a time of famine. You love and appreciate yourself. Your basic value does not change. You can allow others close because you have nothing to hide. When you are down and need a hand up, you can accept it. When you are up, you can lend a hand to another. Your self-value stays the same. Your intrinsic inner worth remains stable because it isn't tied to your outer circumstances.

People with high self-esteem generally make good mates and partners because they are the kind of people who are nice to be around. They appreciate themselves and they appreciate others, too. They value other people's gifts and successes and are generally not jealous of or threatened by them.

Who are the high self-esteemers? Don't look at the outside "package"; look at what's inside. They are the people you feel comfortable and relaxed around. When you are with them, you feel good about yourself. These people inspire you to trust both them and yourself.

You might be asking, "If I want a partner with high self-esteem, does that mean that I have to be willing to give up the creature comforts like money, status and nice things?" My answer is, "Not necessarily." It's just that you are not going to look for those outer trappings. You are going to look for the inner qualities.

Think of it this way: When you ask for a gift, you don't usually specify how the gift is to be wrapped. It's not the wrapping you are interested in having, it's the gift — what's inside the wrapping. Whether the gift is presented in a brown paper bag or in silver paper with a satin bow, the value of the gift remains the same. Certainly, a beautiful package may enhance the experience of receiving the gift, but it doesn't change its value. Conversely, a beautifully wrapped package with nothing inside is a great disappointment and has little or no value to us.

When single people are looking for their ideal mates, they should first decide on the inner qualities they want their partner to have. They should put a lot of focus on the inner qualities, the gift, and only a little focus on the outer circumstances, the wrapping. In other words, it's important to specify the gift, not the wrapping. If Mr./Ms. Right happens to come in a great package, that's a bonus.

How do you find the high-esteemers? Become one! Work diligently on yourself to work through old hurts, increase your self-esteem and become fully the person you were meant to be.

In relationships, like attracts like — so you will draw to yourself the people whose self-esteem matches yours.

What you become will ultimately attract all that you want.[1]

[1] Ronald Reynolds, The Magic of Goals (Laguna Hills, CA: Discovery Publications, 1979).

"It's not too much to expect to be the most important person in someone's life"

— *Author Unknown*

Chapter 2

Bart and Tina — A Love Story

"Bart is the kind of guy most women would love to marry. Thoughtful and sensitive, he's the successful owner of an engineering consulting business," wrote *The Indianapolis Star* when he was interviewed after completing our singles course.

I liked Bart from the first night of class. I could tell right away that he was a caring person who thought deeply about things. The number one thing on Bart's mind at that time was to learn how to have a successful, enduring love relationship. At 35, Bart was still single because he wanted to be sure he knew how to choose the right person and that he had the right skills to not only start but to maintain a satisfying marital partnership. Unlike his parents who divorced bitterly when he was 9 years old, Bart wanted an "until death do us part" marriage.

Shortly after the class session in which we discussed personality styles using the venerable Myers-Briggs Type Indicator, Bart referred a female friend, Tina, to participate in the next Myers-Briggs workshop. I liked Tina instantly, too. The next time I saw Bart, I told him how much I liked her. Then, without any warning, I heard myself saying to him, "Bart, you ought to marry that woman."

Oops! I hadn't intended to tell him. But there it was — out in the open. As we discussed the reasons for my feelings, Bart shared that he liked Tina a lot, too. However, there was a complication. Tina was one of his employees. He didn't want to risk losing "a wonderful employee" if they dated and it didn't work out. Further, since his company was quite small, he didn't want the other employees to know they were dating because of the complications inherent in that situation.

Bart was in a tough spot. He successfully maintained his boundary about not dating Tina while he completed the singles course. During this time, they continued to be good friends and to develop their relationship in after-hours conversations. Later, Bart and Tina began to meet for breakfast on Saturday mornings. Since it was Bart's custom to treat each of his employees to one-on-one social outings from time to time, he figured no one would get suspicious if they saw them having breakfast together.

The Saturday morning breakfasts continued. They started dating, and were married a year later. Tina continues to work for his company, so Bart still has his wonderful employee and now has an equally wonderful wife as well.

In his letter telling me of the marriage, Bart wrote, "Please pass along my encouragement to your class members. Satisfying, fulfilling relationships are out there for those willing to learn, examine themselves, and apply new skills."

Lesson #2

Take the Time to Get Yourself Ready from the Inside Out

"It's a great day in our lives when we realize that we are not the general manager of the universe."[1]

In fact, there is only one corner of the universe we can be certain of improving — ourselves.

Those of us who are single and looking for a partner tend, quite naturally, to focus our energies outward in our search for Mr. or Ms. Right. We look high and low for that person. We network, answer personal ads, accept blind dates and even hire dating services to help us find the person we seek. Sometimes we are successful, but generally we are not. At least not in the early stages of our quest, and that's because we've got the cart before the horse. We are not yet ready to be successfully outer focused.

The Importance of Healing

When we are single and unattached, the first task before us on the road to finding our ideal life partner is to heal from the last relationship we were in. And that may take a while.

Whether it was a long marriage or a short romance, the last relationship we were in affected us in various ways. So our first task after it ends is to assess how we were changed by it. Some of the effects are no doubt positive, and some are negative. That's got to be sorted out first and may be difficult to do right away, because we are still in the "undertow" of that former relationship.

---

[1] Author unknown.

This sorting is similar to the process of moving to a new city when we have to decide what to take, what to give away or sell and what to throw out. And, let's face it, the most difficult part about moving is not really the physical labor involved but the mental labor — all the decisions that we have to make.

Since everything that happens to us happens for our learning, our next task is to figure out what the lessons are that we are meant to learn from this recently ended relationship. The lesson(s) might be, for example, that we need to be more selective in our choice of partners, or to be more prudently generous with our resources, or to take more time in the early stages of relationships.

How long does this take? That depends on how much direct focus and attention we pay to this phase and how soon we do so. The sooner and more directly we focus on it, the more quickly our work is done, and the sooner we can move on. The longer we avoid it by focusing instead on our job or our children or the quest for a new partner or starting a new relationship, the longer it takes. Our work just waits until we are ready to do it. Like dirty laundry, it's no easier to do if it's been sitting around for a while. In fact, it's likely to be a real distraction to us and a turn — off to any new partner.

Birds of a feather flock together, and the same holds true for people. Like attracts like. We feel comfortable and at ease with people who share the same values we do.

Until we have healed from the negative effects of former partners, our values are more or less in flux. We are too out-of-sorts to be truly ourselves or to be very clear about the qualities we are looking for in a partner. As a result, it's difficult for new people to get an accurate reading on who we are and what we stand for.

Relationships started during this transition time are often between two people who are both in the same place, i.e., in transition and avoiding his or her own work. This is a recipe for relationship disaster. It is definitely not the way to begin a healthy, enduring life partnership.

At this stage of disengagement, good friends, a good counselor and a good support group are better for us than a new love.

Do it now or do it later, but there's no way to avoid this work to collect ourselves.

Although the task may be difficult and/or time-consuming, the benefits make it worthwhile. Once our work is done, we experience a tremendous and inevitable increase in our self-esteem. Positive energy radiates naturally out of us and draws the attention of others to us. We don't have to do anything at this point. It just happens. Other people with equally high self-esteem are drawn to us and we to them. We become homing beacons for each other.

And this is how we ultimately find our Mr. or Ms. Right.

In the end, what we become finally attracts all that we want.[1]

---

[1] Reynolds, The Magic of Goals.

"To love and be loved in return is one of life's greatest blessings."

— *Amy Owens*

Chapter 3

Mike and Lisa – A love Story

His heart was broken and he didn't understand what he had done wrong. Sixty-five years old and widowed a year earlier, Mike was confused about dating and relationships when he came to see me for private coaching.

Mike was a man who had retired after two separate careers, one as a naval officer and another in business. Mike and Joanne had been married 45 years when he took his second retirement to care for her as she was dying of cancer.

Joanne died two years later. After her death, Mike, who had been on duty 24/7 for two years, was lost. He no longer had a wife, a job or a purpose for living. He hung around the house for a few months until his brother encouraged him to try getting out socially. Mike, a man with a deep and strong religious background, began attending a church-sponsored singles group in the area. He attended regularly for a couple months enjoying the fellowship of the group and the attention of the ladies. At first, he restricted his socializing to being with groups of men and women after singles programs or church services. That is, until he met Marsha.

From the first time he saw Marsha at a weekend conference of singles, he was interested in being with her and getting to know her. Despite his stated intentions to go slowly, he fell head over heels for Marsha. On their second date, he blurted out that he loved her — not exactly "going slowly" by anyone's measure! The relationship survived the blunder, and they continued to share long distance phone calls and occasional visits and dates with each other. Eventually, Mike could see that he had much more invested in the relationship than Marsha did, so he backed off. When Marsha made no attempt to continue the relationship, he was devastated. That's when Mike came to talk with me.

Reviewing with Mike the relationship with Marsha, it was apparent that it had progressed way too fast to endure. Mike, who had not dated for 46 years, didn't know how to pace a relationship for lasting success. Certainly this was not the way the relationship with Joanne had progressed but "that was the 50's, this is the 90's," he reasoned.

At the time, Mike thought he and Marsha were dating and "courting." Now, when I suggested that they were, in fact, having a fling — a short-lived, intense romance — Mike agreed, relieved that he hadn't done anything wrong.

Mike decided that he had some learning to do and registered for the singles course.

Now, the story gets really interesting.

After completing the singles course, Mike told his friends that he was interested in meeting nice, single women. His social life, which had been non-existent, went from zero to sixty in a heartbeat. Mike went from having no dates and no prospects, to having a full social calendar. Within a month, Mike was introduced to several different women in his age group. He was delighted. The women he met were lovely women, all accomplished in their careers. He had a date every day and some days he had two dates. (After all, when you're retired, you're available for breakfast, lunch and dinner dates!)

In the same magical month, Mike's barber introduced him to one of his wife's friends. Mike gladly accepted the referral and met Lisa, a teacher.

Mike and Lisa hit if off from the beginning. They talked easily with each other and shared a number of common interests including reading, playing Scrabble and travelling.

For Mike, the very best part of their dating relationship was that Lisa cared for him as much as he cared for her. "When I would call Lisa, she would let me know that she was really happy to hear from me. It's not that she was desperate or clingy. She was just very happy to hear from me. She enjoyed my company as much as I enjoyed hers. It was a wonderful feeling."

When Mike first told me about Lisa, I could tell that he was in love. I later told him that he would probably be married in a year. He responded, "If I decide that Lisa is the woman that I want to spend the rest of my life with, what makes you think I'd wait a year to ask her to marry me?"

Loving and being loved in return is truly one of life's greatest blessings.

Lesson #3

Some Relationships are Only Practice Relationships

Practice relationships are not supposed to last forever. They last until we have learned the lessons they were meant to help us learn. Once we have learned the lessons, the practice relationship ends. As my friend, Tom, used to say, "Once you get the message, you hang up the phone."

The reason we have practice relationships is to give us time to get ourselves ready — really, really ready for our ideal or perfect partner, our soul mate. It's our soul mate relationship that is supposed to last.

Think about this: Every relationship we have had has taught us something. Some of our learning took place during the relationship, some after it ended. Then, based on what the lessons were, we made decisions about ourselves, our lives and future partners. If we had not been in those relationships, we probably would not have learned those lessons.

Every time we learn something, we are better for it. As a general rule, we tend, over time, to improve the quality of our lives.

This is easy to see in the area of car buying, for instance. Assuming we always buy the kind of car we can afford, we generally start out with a modest car. Often it is a used car, one that has been in the family for a while. Later, as our income increases, we move up to a better car. Generally, we continue this trend of improving the quality every time we buy a car. The same holds true for where we live, the kind of job we have and even for the kind of relationships (both platonic and romantic) we have. There's a definite upward trend.

Sometimes we want to hurry things, don't we? Why wait until we can afford the luxury car or the big house? We can buy it on credit and "enjoy" it now.

Does it really work that way? Or does the strain of being over-extended take away at least some of the pleasure? If we can afford it, we sleep well at night. If not, we don't. There is no living as good as living within our means.

You Can't Hurry Love

The same holds true for relationships. We start from wherever we are and move up. We begin with whatever skills we have and develop them over time. As we do, we learn new skills and refine those, too. In essence, we practice until we get it right or at least as "right" as we need to in order to attract and keep our soul mate.

Yes, we definitely need practice partners, and that's what the "frogs" in our lives have been. They were people we had "practice" relationships with, and they helped us develop the skills we now have.

We will continue to need practice partners in the future to help us develop and refine the skills necessary for us to live successfully at the high level we truly deserve.

By the way, be assured that your natural level is significantly higher, not lower, than you think it is. In fact, that is exactly the point. It takes all of us some time to realize how great, wonderful and deserving we are.

Let me put it this way — if you are serious about learning a new sport, say tennis, you buy tennis equipment, take lessons, and then you practice. At each level you need practice partners. These are typically people who are at your level or a little above. Over time, because of practicing with them, you move up to or exceed their level of play. Then, rather than quitting tennis, you move on to other partners until you reach the level of play that feels right for you.

In developing relationship skills, we do the same kinds of things. First we buy the equipment — books and tapes. Then we take the lessons: Classes, courses, retreats and workshops. And, finally, we try out a number of practice partners until we find the one who feels just right for us. With that person, our soul mate, we continue to refine our skills and improve our game.

There are no shortcuts for practice. And, we can't buy it on credit. We have to suit up, show up and play our hearts out until we can play the great game we are truly meant to play!

Take Steps to Rebuild Your Social Life

If you, like Mike, have been out of the dating game for an extended period, here are some pointers to guide you in rebuilding your social life.

Step 1: Make as many friends and buddies as possible — first with people of the same sex and then, as you are comfortable, with the opposite sex.

Friends of the same sex are our natural support system and can be especially helpful and supportive in times of crisis.

People of the opposite sex are what I call buddies. These are people who have some of the same interests and hobbies we do. They like to do what we like to do, but they are people with whom we do not have any sexual or romantic attachment or interest. This is absolute. Buddies are friends only. They are like brothers or sisters to us; they are the kind of people with whom we can do "fun stuff".

Bob and I are buddies. When I was single, we enjoyed taking long walks together and talking over our lives as we stepped along. We enjoyed going to movies and out for dinner together. It was so nice to have a confidant, a pal and someone to go out with on Friday or Saturday evening when we didn't have dates.

Step 2: Get involved with group activities that interest you.

Dance lessons are especially good for men since there are usually plenty of women. Group lessons are good for both men and women because dancing allows you to be with people of the opposite sex without the pressure of dating.

Churches can be a good place to get support and to meet people who have the same beliefs. Common values are an important foundation for a healthy relationship.

Classes give you a chance to learn something new even if you don't make friends. Classes that meet a number of times are especially good for introverts who usually take a while to feel comfortable with new people. Choose classes that interest you. If the topic is one both genders are attracted to, so much the better. Consider classes like photography or computers.

Sports, clubs and other activities like camping, cycling, tennis, mixed leagues for volleyball and softball can be good places to meet other active people.

Step 3: Surround yourself with positive people.

Remember that when an "Up" person and a "Down" person get together, the "Down" person pulls the "Up" person down and not vice versa. So look for "Up" people and avoid "Down" ones.

If you feel as though you are a "Down" person, then it's even more important to seek out groups with a positive purpose and "Up" members.

Step 4: Reach out to other people; take the initiative; invite people to do things with you.

Also, learn to "include yourself in" to group activities. Don't wait for an invitation; assume you are included unless you get clear messages to the contrary. Chances are that others want you to participate. If they don't, they will let you know.

Step 5: Learn all you can about healthy relationships and how to create and maintain them.

Learn about the differences between men and women. Learn about dating. Choose to learn in whatever ways are best for you: Reading books, listening to tapes, attending discussion groups, workshops, retreats or classes.

Recommended books include: *Mars & Venus Starting Over* and *Mars & Venus On A Date* by Dr. John Gray; and *The Five Love Languages* by Dr. Gary Chapman. Refer to the Suggested Reading List for additional suggestions.

Step 6: Be patient with yourself, other people and the process.

Great works take time. And, yes, dating now is like it was when you were in high school. There are no shortcuts. You don't get any points for seniority. The best you can hope for is to make better choices now because you are better informed than you were before.

Step 7: Learn about and honor the stages of relationship.

Briefly, the stages are stranger, acquaintance, friend, best friend, intimate, lover, life partner. I recommend taking the time to really get to know someone before you become sexual with them. A good rule of thumb is to spend a minimum of 300 hours with them — talking, playing, talking, working, talking, meeting their friends and talking before you make it to the bedroom. This is probably the one most important piece of information I can offer you about how to increase your chances for creating a healthy, enduring relationship.

If your church's teaching or your personal belief is to postpone being sexual with each other until after marriage, then it's very important that you do so.

There is a fuller discussion of the stages of relationship in Chapter 4.

Step 8: Remember that the Cosmic Dating Service is always working for you.

In this case, like attracts like. So, work to get your own life in order and to become the best you can be. You will attract people who have done the same.

Chapter 4

Debbie and Randy — A Love Story

Debbie started the singles course at the urging of her counselor. The counselor wanted Debbie to begin getting out socially with other singles, and she knew the class would be a safe place for Debbie to do so.

Debbie didn't really want to come to a singles class advertised as being "for singles who are serious about finding life partners." Still in the process of a bitter divorce after 25 years of a painful marriage, she had no intentions of getting married ever again.

A charge nurse who worked evenings, Debbie was an introverted woman who lived a quiet life.

Quiet Debbie had a hobby. Her hobby was something she was passionate about. Her hobby brought fun and solace into her life as she worked to rebuild her life and her self-esteem. Her hobby gave her a place in her life where she could have control and make decisions for herself — things she was not "allowed" to do in her marriage.

Debbie's hobby was playing cards. She loved to play cards. Any game. Any time. Debbie was always game for a game of cards.

Would it surprise you to hear that Debbie even played cards on the Internet? Yes, she did. She played with a regular group. She played every day. The other players were all avid players, too. She formed friendships with some of the other players. One of those players was Randy who lived a thousand miles away.

Debbie's relationship with Randy began on-line while they were playing cards. First they talked while playing cards. Then they chatted with each other on-line. Later they talked by phone. Eventually, they met in person.

The first meeting took place a couple weeks after Debbie started the singles course. Debbie, uneasy about even the idea of dating again, tried not to tell us about it. However, when she came to class, her happiness was written all over her face. The big smile she wore was a dead giveaway!

During the next three months while she completed the singles course, Debbie continued to play cards, e-mail, and chat with Randy. The frequency of their contacts gradually increased until they were talking with each other every day. They became good friends.

After their second in-person visit, Randy told Debbie he wanted to marry her. He asked Debbie to move to where he and his 16-year-old daughter lived.

Debbie said no. It was too soon, and she was not interested in moving anywhere.

The card playing and talks continued, and their friendship deepened.

A few months later, Randy accepted a job transfer. He packed up his home and his daughter and moved to the city where Debbie lived. While Randy and Debbie maintained separate residences, they continued to play cards, talk and get to know each other.

The relationship continued to deepen, and Debbie's trust in Randy grew. She could now begin to imagine that not all men were mean and controlling like her former husband.

A year later, another job transfer moved Randy two hours away. This time Debbie moved with him. The relationship deepened. Debbie, who had never wanted to get married again, began to "consider" becoming engaged to Randy.

Eventually, about three years after they met, Debbie and Randy were married.

Lesson #4

It Takes Time to Develop Healthy, Satisfying, Enduring Relationships

Relationships — all relationships — take time to develop.

Building or creating a relationship is a bit like baking a cake. You need to have all the right ingredients, the right equipment, the right amount of "heat" and enough time to bake it. If you are missing any one of the elements you cannot successfully bake a cake.

You cannot take a cake out of the oven before it's done just because you're in a hurry and can't wait.

If you take a cake out of the oven too soon, you will spoil it. Instead of a yummy treat you will have a gooey, nasty mess, and that's a disappointment. Who needs another disappointment?

When I was a new counselor, my counseling colleague Beverly Freet taught me a great model for understanding how relationships develop. Here's Beverly's model.

An Exercise in Trust

Imagine for a minute that you are flying in a space ship looking back on planet Earth. Imagine that you can see all of the people on the planet. How many people are there? The answer is billions, about six billion right now. How many of those billions of people do you know? Several hundred? Several thousand?

No matter how many people you know, the vast majority of those six billion people are strangers to you, aren't they? Most of the people in the world at any given time are strangers to you.

Now, back on Earth, imagine that you are leaving a sporting arena or concert hall after an event. You are walking through the halls on the way to the exit. Look around at the people. Most of them are strangers, aren't they? As you imagine being there with those strangers, what do you know about them? Don't make any assumptions like, "They are fans." (They may not be fans. They may have come because they are courting business or because someone gave them free tickets.) What you accurately know about these strangers is only what you can see — their clothes, face, hair, etc. So you know very little about them.

What is your trust level with these people? High, low or somewhere in between? That probably depends a lot on how trustful a person you are in general. Most people say their trust level in a situation like this is low or fairly low.

How much time do you spend with these strangers? Very little.

What are your responsibilities toward them? The usual answer is common courtesy. You don't step on their feet, and you don't steal their popcorn.

What are your expectations as far as their behavior towards you? Typically the same: Common courtesy.

Now, let's move from strangers to a smaller group of people Beverly calls acquaintances.

Who are acquaintances? They are typically people you see more than once, like the neighbor who lives across the street, or the group of people who always sit at the table in the corner of the lunch room at work, or people you see in the crowd at church.

What and how much do you know about these acquaintances? Probably not too much — but more than strangers. You might, for instance, know that your neighbor drives a certain kind of car, typically leaves for work about 7:00 in the morning and returns home about 6:00 in the evening, is married (darn!) and has two children.

What's your trust level with acquaintances? Generally about the same or a bit higher than with strangers.

How much time do you spend with them? Generally, very little, if any.

What are your responsibilities toward acquaintances? About the same as strangers. Common courtesy, plus you might do them a small favor, like opening a door or putting your neighbor's mis-delivered mail to their mailbox instead of sending it back through the postal system.

Their responsibilities to you? About the same as you to them.

The next group of people is friends. For the sake of this discussion, I am referring to garden-variety friends, not best friends. A smaller group than the previous two, friends are people you know more about, trust more and spend more time with. Friends are typically people with whom you have one or more interests in common. This kind of friend might be someone you met in a tennis class who is now your doubles partner.

Your responsibilities to this type of friend might be to practice between games, show up on time, pay your own bill and to be friendly. They might do you a favor if it doesn't put them out. You would expect them to do the same in return, wouldn't you?

The next category, a still smaller group, is best friends. These are people you really care about, trust a lot, know a lot about and spend significant amounts of time with. They expect you to be honest and trustworthy and vice versa.

Intimates is the next category of relationships. I am referring to people with whom we are emotionally intimate, not sexually intimate. Emotional intimates can be people of either gender. Our relationships with these people have generally stood the test of time. We have a history with them.

Our intimates know more about us than anyone else does. Our trust level is very high. We feel safe enough to share with them not only our troubles, our hopes and our dreams, but also our fears and the things about ourselves that we don't really like. The intimates in our lives are the people who can give us the feedback we need to have about ourselves but don't want to hear. Somehow, when we hear it from them, it's OK, even helpful. These are the people who will do favors for us even when it's inconvenient or difficult for them to do so. We are willing to do the same for them.

The next smallest category of relationships is lovers. They are intimates with whom we also have a sexual relationship.

Then there are life partners or soul mates. I think of them as lovers with a lifetime commitment.

The final category, the very smallest, is the relationship we have with ourselves. It's the relationship we have always been in, and it's the most intimate one of all.

All relationships, regardless of gender, follow this natural progression: Stranger, acquaintance, friend, best friend, intimate, lover, life partner. Obviously, most relationships plateau in the early stages (stranger, acquaintance, friend) with very few making it to the later stages (intimate, lover, life partner).

Take a minute to think about this information before reading further.

Here's a crucial question: How long would you say it took you to develop the relationships with your best friends and intimates?

A couple days? A couple weeks? Several months? Longer? Most people say it took a long time — years.

As single people, what kind of relationships do we want most? The ones that take the longest to build: intimate, lover and life partner. And what's our tendency when we meet someone we really like? To rush rather than taking our time and allowing the relationship to develop, grow and deepen.

We all want to believe that a romantic relationship can be intimate from the first glance, i.e., "love at first sight". And, we want to believe that because it feels good we should do it. We'd also like to believe that we are somehow special and don't really need to take our time. Or perhaps we are afraid of losing this great person and need to grab them before they get away. These are all sincere beliefs but faulty ones.

It Takes Time

Great works take time. A great romantic partnership takes time.

How much time? Enough time to progress from stranger/ acquaintance to intimate/lover. Although it may take years to do that with a person of the same sex, couples can usually do so more quickly. My rule of thumb is to spend a minimum of 300 hours getting to know each other and developing the relationship before becoming lovers.

Most people who have learned this model agree that 300 hours is a very short amount of time considering what we are trying to accomplish. Those who have tried it have been glad they did.

As in Chapter 3, I encourage those whose church teaching or personal belief is to postpone sexual activity until after marriage to stand by those principles. It does not hurt a relationship to move slowly. It's moving too fast that puts it in jeopardy.

Let me give you an example. In 1995, when I presented this model to the students in the very first series of the singles course, I got a strong reaction from one of the students.

Karen, a college professor with a Ph.D., waited until I finished describing the stages and then erupted with emotion. She said emphatically, "That's it. Now, I know why my marriages failed — neither one of my two ex-husbands was ever my best friend!" Karen went on to say, "Everyone is in such a hurry to get to be lovers that they rush through the first stages. They think and hope they are doing it right, but they're not. They're hoping to make a beeline into the middle of the grid. When they rush, they don't make it into the middle at all. Instead, they veer off and are projected out of the grid. They hoped to create a love affair. Instead, they created an aberration. It's not really a love relationship at all."

Rather than building and enjoying a healthy enduring love affair, the couple who rushes has a fling — a passionate, intense physical interaction that has little or no soul connection.

Flings are, by definition, short-lived. That's because the couple has built a house without a foundation. It's just a matter of time until it falls down around them.

Flings typically last from "one-night stands" to several weeks, but they do not endure. They cannot last because they are fundamentally flawed. Flings are largely sexual experiences, and sexual experiences are intense. Because the couple has not first built a fireproof container to handle the sexual fire, their sexual activity burns up the relationship. My student, Bill, calls this the "Rush-Crash-Burn" phenomenon. This is what happened with Mike and Marsha.

The fireproof container I am talking about is the relationship, the strong partnership that results from building a personal connection stage by stage, as Beverly Freet describes. That is the kind of connection that Mike built with Lisa whom he later married. It's the same kind of connection that all ten of these couples created.

What do couples do for 300 hours? They talk, walk and go to movies. They enjoy dinners, concerts and shows together. They talk, attend weddings, birthday parties and holiday gatherings. They work and play and talk with each other. They meet each other's family. And, yes, they even play cards together!

Do people actually keep track of the hours? Some do, some don't. Engineers and CPA's often do. Most others don't count up the hours until they are close to becoming sexual with each other. Then, they sit down and reconstruct the time they have spent together. Usually they find they are very close to 300 hours.

Does the time spent on the telephone count? Only if you are in a long-distance relationship where phone time is relationship time.

Who sets the pace for the relationship, and whose job is it to keep it from going too fast? Both partners.

I suggest sharing the information about the stages and the 300-hour rule of thumb on the first or second date. You can share it as something you've learned that you think is a good idea and ask your date for his or her opinion. Since many first dates include a meal, there is usually a square cocktail napkin on the table for you to use to draw the "boxes in boxes" diagram.

If your date is just looking for a fling, they won't see any value in waiting. But, if an enduring partnership is what they want, they will see and acknowledge the wisdom of the model.

Here's how my student, Carolyn, used the stages model. "The sequences and progression of a relationship were very important information to keep the relationship flowing at the appropriate speed. I constantly asked myself, 'Would I do this with someone I just met?' It was amazing how well this worked for me. I gauged each step of our relationship as to what stage we were in at the time. Keeping our interaction in sync with the stages was very important to the progress of our friendship. All of the initial steps — going from mere acquaintances to becoming friends, then best friends, to becoming intimate — led us to the passion we now share with each other. We have built a foundation of trust and security that we can carry with us through our life together."

More Questions to Ask Yourself

Take some time to reflect on these questions:

1. What one idea presented in this model was the most important to you?

2. Overall, are you aware of having relationships in all of these different categories?

3. Has it been your pattern to rush through the get-acquainted stages of a relationship? Or have you typically taken your time, moving slowly from one stage to the next?

4. Does your level of commitment generally tend to match the stage of the relationship? Do you tend to over-commit or under-commit?

5. Are there any "adjustments" you would like to make in current relationships?

6. What changes, if any, would you like to make in your approach to future relationships?

"There is a time for everything and a season for every activity under heaven."

— Ecclesiastes 3:1

Stages of Relationship

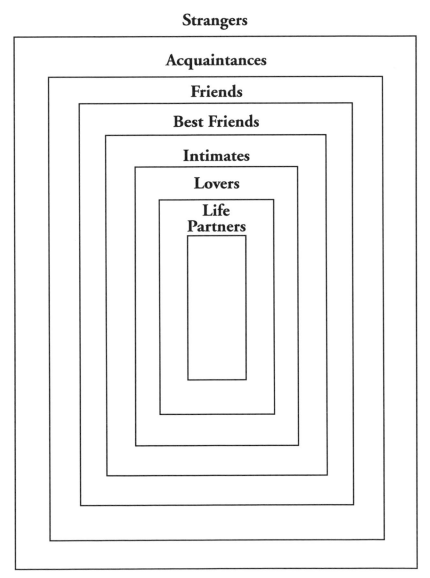

Strangers

Acquaintances

Friends

Best Friends

Intimates

Lovers

Life
Partners

Healthy relationships, regardless of gender, develop in this way.

"What we become will finally attract all that we want."
— *Ronald Reynolds*

Chapter 5

Susi and Ron — A Love story

Susi was widowed at 53 after thirty-three years of marriage. She had always thought of herself as strong and independent, but the death of her husband brought her to her knees. She was devastated by the loss of the companionship and support her husband had provided all those years.

"For about six months," she said, "I threw myself into working and staying busy. I figured if I worked enough and stayed busy enough, I wouldn't have to feel the pain. That way I didn't have to admit that he was really gone." Later, Susi began to see a counselor who helped her grieve her losses.

Next, Susi, who at first had clung to her married friends, began to socialize with a group of five other single women. One of the five was also a widow; the other four were divorced. Susi had a lot of fun with these women and gradually got her life back in balance.

About a year after her husband's death, Susie went out with the group for dinner. At the restaurant, she met a school friend from her hometown 20 miles away. This friend later shared the news about Susi with another former schoolmate, Ron, also recently widowed. The friend suggested that Ron give Susi a call because they had a lot in common and would enjoy each other.

When Ron called Susi a few weeks later, they talked easily by phone for quite a while. After agreeing to go to dinner with him, Susi recalls thinking to herself, "I'm going on a date. Now, what do I do?"

At dinner, they "spent hours and hours talking." They began to see each other every weekend, but there was no physical chemistry — no bells or whistles. Susi decided that "Ron is going to be just a blessed, valuable friend."

Ron's circle of married friends embraced her, and they enjoyed an active social life together. Their friendship grew very slowly.

Ron was the first to realize that something more might come of their relationship, but he was very respectful of Susi's need to warm up to the idea. After a couple months of dating, he told Susi that he very much wanted to give her a hug but wanted to wait until she was ready.

Ron later confessed that he had written down every date they had and the amount of time they spent together. "I waited 174 hours for that first hug," he told her.

About this time, Susi heard about my singles course from her widowed girlfriend. She enrolled and attended the first several classes of the course. After the class in which students define their Mr./Ms. Right, Susi went home and gave some serious thought to the topic.

She later told me, "That was when I decided that Ron, the man I was dating, was my Mr. Right. If I hadn't taken the course, I wouldn't have been as perceptive about what was going on in the relationship with Ron. Because we didn't have instant chemistry, I figured we would only ever be friends. But after that class, I decided that he was the man I was looking for. We got engaged shortly after and were married a year later."

Lesson #5

It Is Important to Define Who You Are and Whom You Are Looking For

Have you ever asked someone to go to the grocery store to buy something for you but not told them what to buy? Probably not.

How is someone supposed to know what to get for you if you don't tell them? How can you tell them if you don't know what it is that you want?

Most of the singles I talk with say they know what they want in a mate. However, when I ask them to tell me what they are looking for, their answers are often pretty vague or are stated in negative terms:

"I want a companion."

"I want someone to have fun with."

"I don't want to die alone."

"I don't want someone I have to take care of."

If I were your guardian angel and you gave me one of those answers, I would have a hard time knowing what to give you.

Sometimes, though, people's answers are too specific or are unrealistic:

> "I want a wealthy woman who is an artist, sews her own clothes, has long, straight, brown hair, brown eyes, weighs 105# and is beautiful without make-up."

> "I want someone who doesn't have any baggage."

Oh, try to fill those orders!

When we are searching for Mr./Ms. Right, it's important to have specific, realistic criteria which allow some "wiggle room." As we discussed in Chapter 1, it's important to be specific about the gift but flexible about the package it comes in.

Just as it's a good idea to make a shopping list before you go to the grocery store, it's a good idea to make a list of what you are looking for in a mate before you begin shopping for him or her.

Here's another way to think about this. Choosing a mate is a lot like buying a car. You don't want to buy a car in a fever with all the risks inherent in that — paying too much, buying more car than you need, getting "seduced" by gimmicks or being fast-talked into a deal that's not right for you — so you take some time to think about what you want. You get very specific about the car you want to buy.

The Car-Buying Process

Step 1: You decide on the main purpose for having the vehicle. Will it be to transport you as a business executive, a parent, a gardener or a sports enthusiast?

Step 2: You decide on the must-haves, the non-negotiables like front-wheel drive, power accessories and a sunroof.

Step 3: You decide on the negotiables — the equipment you are willing to pay extra for.

Step 4: You decide on the luxuries — the bonus items that would be nice if included in the package but which you are not willing to pay extra for.

Making Your Mr./Ms. Right List

Step 1: Get clear about why you want someone to share your life. What purpose will this person fill in your life? Is it to start a family, to finish raising a family or to enjoy the "empty nest" years with you? Are you looking for companionship, intellectual stimulation, a meal ticket, a trophy for your arm or someone to launch a business with you?

Step 2: List all the traits and characteristics you would like this person to have. Then, pare the list down to three to five items that become your non-negotiables.

Step 3: From among the leftover items from Step 2, choose your "negotiables".

Step 4: Allow yourself to dream of the most wonderful traits you can imagine and write them down, too.

Tah Dah! You have your Mr./Ms. Right list.

Although you may be able to complete the list in a matter of minutes, put your list aside for a while — maybe a couple days or a couple weeks. Then, review it, adding and changing items until it seems just right for you. (It doesn't have to please anyone but you.)

Finally, I suggest you type the list and post it somewhere you will see it often. If you live alone, the refrigerator is a good spot. Other good spots are in your daily planner, in your Bible or nightstand, or on your computer as a screensaver.

"What if someone else sees it on my refrigerator?" Well, by the time a date has time to hang around your kitchen reading what's on your fridge, isn't it time he or she knew who you are looking for and what's important to you?

"Should I show it to someone I'm dating?" Not necessarily. It's a good idea to have a number of conversations — beginning with your first date — about what's important to you and where you see yourself going in the future. But it is not necessary to show your dates the list. Use your list to keep you on target as my student, Deborah, did.

In a letter dated about a year after she completed the singles course, Deborah wrote: "I just wanted to drop you a note to let you know how much I enjoyed the 'Advanced Relationship Strategies' class for singles. Early last summer, I met a wonderful man and fell in love...We met at one of the Sunday night singles dances and just 'clicked' right away...There's such a wonderful amount of harmony between us.

"I still have my 'soul mate' list on the refrigerator. That list is probably the single most important thing I took from the class. It helped me to get really clear about my priorities and to stay focused on them, especially when I found myself attracted to someone who, though nice, was not appropriate for me. That new-found ability to `pass' on an inappropriate relationship helped me to be `open' when Mr. Right came into view — and I'm so glad!"

The following is a sample list that might give you some ideas about what you want to include on your list.

His/Her role in my life:

- ♥ Companion — a love receptacle for me who cherishes me in return

- ♥ Everyday presence in my life

- ♥ Provider of intellectual stimulation

- ♥ Comfortable and interesting travel companion

- ♥ Co-creator with me in projects of many types

- ♥ Participates in and mirrors my personal and spiritual growth

- ♥ Active participant in growing our relationship

- ♥ Satisfying sex partner

Traits:

- ❤ Is spiritually evolved

- ❤ Has good relationship and communication skills

- ❤ Sees our relationship as a top priority

- ❤ Is available and wants a relationship with me now

- ❤ Is crazy about me and tells me so

- ❤ Is a non-smoker

- ❤ Takes good care of him/herself physically

- ❤ Enjoys food, fine dining and cooking

- ❤ Will be genuinely supportive of me in any situation

- ❤ Cares about my good and my success as much as his/her own

- ❤ Values people, travel, deep conversation and personal growth

- ❤ Enjoys music, especially classical

- ❤ Operates with bottom-line honesty with him/herself, me and others

- ❤ Is committed to our relationship

- ❤ Views me as his/her best friend and partner

- ❤ Is a gentle, attentive lover

- ❤ Is intelligent and intellectually curious

♥ Has a sense of humor and laughs easily at him/herself

♥ Can and does say, "I'm sorry."

♥ Cares about his/her appearance and mine

♥ Is generous with his/her money and time

♥ Is physically demonstrative, loving and affectionate

♥ Is a genuinely happy person

"Your talk talks and your walk talks, but your walk talks more than your talk talks."

— *Author Unknown*

Chapter 6

Anna and Dan — A Love Story

After 10 years of marriage, Anna had been divorced for seven years when she decided she needed to make some changes in her life. "I was at a point where I was willing to try new things and make some big changes. I had friends at the plant where I worked who were taking a course that helped single adults build long-lasting relationships. They talked about how great this was and suggested I try it. I decided it might be time for me to do something like this, so I made the decision to enroll," Anna said.

Little did Anna know this decision would change her life.

When I first met Anna, I was struck by what a beautiful person she was inside and out. At one of the first class meetings, Anna told me she intended to complete the course although she was very skeptical that she could find a really nice man. I told her, "I believe the man you are looking for is out there, and he's looking for you right now." (I say this to a lot of people, because I believe it. And, I believe it applies to you, too.)

In describing the benefits she received from the course, Anna says, "The skills I took away from this program not only helped me to understand more about building long-lasting relationships, they also helped me in everyday life. I was able to deal and cope with life's challenges overall in a much better way. I also gained a totally different perspective on meeting new people. I learned how to meet people that are right for me specifically.

"One of the best things this program did for me was increase the amount of self-confidence I had. I became a confident person. You carry yourself differently when you have confidence, and people do notice this. It really enables you to draw quality people into your life. I left the program a totally different person," she added.

In the midst of taking the course, Anna's new relationship skills were put to the test. Out of the blue, she got a phone call from Dan, a man she had been engaged to after high school. They had eventually gone their separate ways and married other people. He told her that his marriage had ended, and that he had thought about her on and off over the years. They decided to get together to talk and catch up.

Their talks led to dates and a month later they fell in love with each other again. "After my divorce, the only consolation I could imagine was that there was something better waiting down the road for me. I was so surprised Dan came back — it was almost like a prayer that was answered. I finally saw the light at the end of the tunnel," Anna says of reuniting with Dan.

Filled with self-confidence, Anna was clear about herself and what she wanted in a mate. "Because of my self-confidence, I was able to voice my thoughts and feelings to Dan and to get our new relationship started in the right way," she added.

After a few months of dating, both Anna and Dan felt as though they had been given a second chance. Dan, realizing that second chances don't come around very often, proposed to Anna. They were married a few months later on New Year's Eve with the clear intent of starting a new year and a new life together.

Lesson #6

It's OK to Take a Vacation from Dating

"I'm just so tired of dating. I feel like giving up. I just want to curl up on my couch and forget about it."

Have you ever said that? I have.

There is no doubt about it, dating is hard work. You have to go places and make contacts so you can meet eligible dating candidates. Then, you have to screen those candidates, make plans, and go out on dates.

Most often, you find out that your dates are not who you are looking for. In the meantime, you have spent time, money and a bunch of energy. You have worked hard to show your best side — to be accommodating, interesting, attractive and fun. But, you've come home empty-handed. If you were a fisherman and came home with no catch, you would be upset.

As a fisherman with no catch, you'd get sympathy and support. But when you're a single-but-looking person, what do you get? Well, best case scenario, if you have a great support group of single friends, you'll get sympathy and support. If you don't yet have this kind of network, you're probably not going to talk about your disappointment. "They wouldn't understand..."

Well, it is normal to run out of enthusiasm for dating from time to time. And, as a single person, it's important to have a safe network of supportive people.

And, it's OK to take a time-out from dating for a while. Please notice I said, "For a while." I'm not saying you can quit forever. Just for a while.

You may ask, "How do I take a time-out? What do I do when I'm taking a time-out?" Here are some things to consider.

The most important thing about a time-out is that it's a time to rest and nurture your spirit. This is a time when your spirit needs attention, and pampering. What you do to provide those things for yourself will vary from person to person and from time to time.

Before we go any further, I want to make clear that taking a time-out when you need one is one of the most important things you can do to further your search for your soul mate. You will draw him or her into your life when you are in a good space with yourself.

One more thing: Taking time-outs is not just a good idea. It's mandatory. Without taking rest breaks when you need them, you may jeopardize your health and your spirit by making poor decisions simply because you were tired and not thinking straight.

A dating vacation can take any form you choose. I suggest you sit quietly in a favorite place and figure out what you need and then set about providing it for your precious self.

Sometimes, you may need to be alone. Other times you may need to be with people — safe people. Let your inner voice tell you which it is.

Ideas for "Vacations" from Dating

Here are some ways I have spent my "dating vacations". Maybe some of these ideas will work for you.

I used to take a "veg" day about once a month. On a Saturday or Sunday, I made plans to stay at home and in bed. I'd get up only to eat and then go back to bed to sleep, to read magazines or a mystery novel, or to do crossword puzzles. I'd take a shower late in the afternoon, change into fresh pajamas, eat supper and watch TV until bedtime. The next day I felt as though I'd been away for a weekend vacation, without packing a suitcase.

Sometimes I'd spend the weekend working alone in my yard and garden, soaking up the beauty of nature.

Occasionally, I would take myself out alone to dinner and a movie — even on a Saturday night.

Another spirit-nurturing routine I had was a monthly full-body massage. My appointment time was late on Friday afternoon. After the massage, I'd stop on the way home to pick up Chinese carry-out for supper. When I got home, I'd give my dog a quick walk and then curl up on my couch until bedtime. I always slept like a baby on massage nights and felt relaxed and rested the next day.

My favorite time-out was to take a solo vacation at the beach about every two years. I didn't "do" anything but eat, sleep and watch the ocean. Ah, for me that is the ultimate renewal of spirit.

So, you want to take a vacation from dating? Go ahead! Enjoy yourself. Just remember that vacations last for a while, not forever.

Chapter 7

Becky and John — A Love Story

"When John and I got married, I was truly the blushing bride," says Becky.

"My participation in the singles course got me focused back on my life — on what I wanted and how to get it for myself. I decided that as soon as I got my house paid off, I was going to buy myself an all-brick home with blueberry bushes and a place to have a garden and flowers.

"Although I am pretty introverted, I learned the value of networking. I also learned that I didn't have to accept a man's attention just because he wanted to give it to me. Although I still wanted to be married again, I decided I was satisfied with myself and my life. If it took forever to find Mr. Right, then so be it," Becky adds.

Divorced for two years after a 31-year marriage, Becky was 49 when she started the singles course. Believing that "God is the giver of second chances," Becky knew it was important for her to adhere to her church's teaching and to abstain from sex before marriage.

Becky met John at a dance and liked him right away. They met and danced together a couple more times before John called to ask her for a date. "He had to call and ask me out four times before I was free to go out with him. It impressed me that he would keep trying so many times," Becky recalls.

On their first date, Becky was up front with John about maintaining sexual abstinence, and John was OK with this. Over the ensuing months, John and Becky got to know each other very well as they talked and played cards across her dining room table.

One day John offered to show her his house but Becky declined. "I am interested in getting to know you. I want to like you because of you, not because of what you have," she told him.

When one of her sons was graduating from college out-of-state, Becky wanted to have a male escort, as she knew her ex-husband and his new wife would be there. Instead of asking John, Becky decided to tough it out. John surprised her, however, by asking to go along on the trip, which he did. The way he eased himself into the extended family group amazed and delighted Becky.

It was after she returned home from that trip that Becky rediscovered her Mr. Right list in her bedside table. "When I read it over, I realized that John was everything I had asked for in the list."

Becky and John became engaged soon after. When they met with her pastor for pre-marriage counseling sessions, they were each asked what had attracted them to the other. John's response was, "Becky's high moral standards." It was then that Becky learned that both of John's former wives had been unfaithful to him. With Becky, John knew he had a woman he loved and whom he could trust.

They married about 18 months after they met. When Becky moved into his home after the wedding, John gave her free reign to rearrange and decorate the house to her liking, which she did.

Almost two years later, Becky and John are gratefully happy for their second chance.

By the way, Becky and John live in his all-brick house that is surrounded by blueberry bushes, a one-acre vegetable garden, and "flower beds you wouldn't believe."

Lesson #7

Keep Your Standards High

"Maybe I am being too picky." "My mother and my friends say I'm being too picky..."

I hear these comments frequently. The speaker is usually someone who has very recently been hurt or disappointed in a relationship. Or, they are in the middle of a long dry spell and their hope is running low. In an honest attempt to fix the problem, they are willing to lower their standards. WRONG, very wrong!

Why? If you think about it for a moment, how is lowering your standards going to get you something better? Certainly, what you want is something better, not worse than you have.

In matters of the heart, with in most things in life, good sense logic applies. If you want something better, you need to be willing to pay the price for it.

If you want a diamond, you have to be willing to pay the price a diamond costs. This is not the time nor the situation to be bargain hunting or flea market shopping! You need to have your good duds on, your money in your pocket and be heading for the upscale shop that specializes in the kind of item you want.

All right, there is such a thing as a diamond-in-the-rough. But take a minute and dissect that one: we're not talking about a "sloppy" diamond, are we?

No, we are talking about something that is a gem of high value on the inside. And, isn't that what you're after? Yes, there's work to be done to retrieve the inside value, but it's worth it, isn't it?

Think of Yourself As A Gem

Let's shift our focus for a moment away from the person we're looking for and turn it back onto ourselves. We are also diamonds-in-the-rough. We are also works in progress. We, too, have potential beyond our present circumstances. We also have goodness and value that may not be immediately apparent.

Let's twist this a bit more. How would you feel if your Mr./Ms. Right expected to find you at a garage sale? Wouldn't you be insulted? Wouldn't you want to let him/her know, in no uncertain terms, that you are more valuable? Garage sale? No way. "Look for me in the U.S. Treasury where the one-of-a-kind gold pieces are kept," you'd say. And rightly so.

You are a magnificent piece of work. One of a kind. "An irrepeatable miracle of God," as the singles pastor in Michigan says. In all of time, you are the only you. There never was and never will be another YOU. Forget special, you are absolutely unique.

Should you lower your standards? Absolutely not. You should RAISE them! After all, you are looking for a match for a one of a kind, unique, irrepeatable miracle. Garage sale? No way. Flea market? Don't think so. Bar? Probably not.

Think about this for a moment: Where do you want to be discovered? On your couch wrapped in doubt, fear and self-pity? Or, out and about where the "diamonds" are — at a bookstore, with trusted friends, walking your dog, working out, in church, playing sports, attending a concert, participating in a self-improvement class?

It's your job to smooth your own rough edges and to polish yourself so Mr./Ms. Right will see you as the gem you really are.

As you're working to get yourself ready, sustain your hope with this thought:

> It's not too much to expect to be the most
> important person in someone's life.

"The work we do on ourselves is the potential
we bring to relationship."
— *Steven and Ondrea Levine*

Chapter 8

Barbara and John — A Love Story

Barbara had been maried and divorced a few times by the time she was 38 years old. That was when she decided to figure out why she kept drawing abusive, alcoholic men into her life.

Barb started counseling — in earnest. From her vantage point, both her life and the lives of her children depended on her getting herself straightened out.

Barb also began attending church. She found a pastor and a church community that embraced her as the cherished soul she is.

The renovation of her life took Barb nearly a decade.

During that time, she raised her children alone, made a number of geographical moves, and built an impressive resume as a tool and die maker. She bought a beautiful suburban home and upgraded the kitchen with custom-made cabinets she built and installed by herself. She bought and learned to pilot a large sailboat. She developed an ever-expanding social network of men and women.

When Barb looks back at that decade, she cites learning to be OK with being alone as her biggest accomplishment. "I learned to be happy in my own company. I didn't need anybody to be able to have a good time. I could, and did, have happy times all by myself." This was quite a remarkable feat, given how naturally extroverted and social she is.

Barb is someone who has never met a stranger. To Barb, every person is a potential friend and potential source of fun. And, oh, how Barb likes to have fun — joking, teasing, laughing, playing. When Barb enters a room, you know it. Within moments of her arrival, you feel her presence. Sometimes it's because the room is now standing on its end. Other times, you notice a group of people across the room that seems to be having a lot of fun. In the center of that group, instigating the fun, you will find Barb.

Along the way, Barb had an on and off relationship with another man who was not good for her. When she started the singles course, that five-year relationship was temporarily in the "off" mode.

In the singles class, Barb learned what she still needed to understand about creating healthy relationships. She began to see why boundaries are needed in relationships and how to set and maintain them. Most of all, she learned that she had a right to have boundaries for herself in all her relationships. Barb says she also learned to take her time and start new relationships slowly.

Barb's self-confidence increased, and she freed herself from the on/off relationship.

About three months after completing the singles course, Barb began to date a man whom she met at work. An industrial machine salesman, John was supervising the installation of a large piece of new equipment in the area of the plant where Barb worked. John was in the plant on a daily basis for a week or more and then in touch with Barb by phone to follow up on the progress of the machine.

Although they had met in the plant a year earlier, this time something was different. From John's perspective, Barb was different. At the time, he wasn't exactly sure what the difference was, and he had no idea what had caused the change. He noticed the change, and he liked it. He asked Barb to go out with him. She accepted.

Recalling that time in their relationship, Barb and John both say they knew something special was going on between them. Both were committed, however, to going slowly.

One of the things that Barb especially liked about John was that he didn't need her. "He wants me in his life, but he doesn't need me. He can get along fine without me, but I add to his happiness in the same way that dessert adds to the enjoyment of a good meal."

Barb and John dated for a year before becoming engaged and married a few months later.

Married almost two years now, Barb and John are having the time of their lives. They have bought a three-acre lot on which they have personally built a large barn. They plan to begin building their new home on the same property soon.

Barb says John helps keep her focused and grounded. John says Barb lights up his life. Their life together is filled with love, laughter and fun.

Lesson #8

Build Your Dream Life While You Are
Waiting for Mr./Ms. Right

As The Singles Coach I am frequently asked, "What do I have to do to meet my soul mate?" or "When will I meet my Mr. (or Ms.) Right?"

Those are fair questions. I can remember giving voice to them quite often. "What?" and "When?" became mantras for me. Does this sound familiar?

In matters of the heart, like-attracts-like. We tend to draw to us people whose lives are in the same general "shape" as ours. For example, a person in transition from a job or a relationship will tend to attract others who are also in transition. People with money or family problems will often attract others with money or family problems. The converse also tends to be true.

People who are settled into single life in a happy, complete way will attract other settled, happy, complete singles. Most of us would like our Mr. or Ms. Right to be settled, happy and complete. So, our task is to order our lives until we are happy and complete, too.

My wise friend, Joe, taught me that in order to attract your equal, "you first have to create the kind of lifestyle that you would like to have with that partner. you should begin:

- Driving the kind of car you would like to drive

- Wearing the kind of clothes you would like to wear

- Eating the kind of food you would like to eat

- Traveling to the kind of places you would like to travel to

- Participating in the kind of activities you would like to participate in

- Living in the kind of house you would like to live in when you are partnered

"Then, you will attract the kind of person who likes those things too."

Joe's very logical, isn't he? And, he's right. It makes sense that people with similar likes are also apt to like each other. This doesn't mean they will like each other, but the chances are definitely higher.

Build Your Dream List

Here's an exercise to help you get started. On a blank sheet of paper, write these headings down the left side of the page leaving about an inch of blank space between them:

Finances

Work

Mental/emotional health

Religion/spiritual values

Physical health

Family/home

Social

Appearance

Hobbies

Other

Next, picture your Mr. or Ms. Right. What are the "qualifications" you would like him or her to have in each of these categories? Be specific. Don't worry about being "too picky." You deserve the best you can imagine for yourself.

If you aren't sure which category to put something in, just pick the heading that makes the most sense to you.

When you have finished writing your qualifications for Mr./Ms. Right, review what you have written.

Make sure you have been specific and that you have stated your requirements for them in positive terms. That is, you have written down what you want rather than what you don't want. Make changes as needed. For example, if you have written, "Doesn't smoke", change that entry to "Is a non-smoker" or "Is smoke-free." Rather than saying, "Is not a workaholic", write: "Has a healthy work ethic", or "Has a good balance between work life and personal life".

The idea is to state what we do want rather than what we don't want.

Imagine what would happen if we asked someone to go to the grocery store for us and only told him or her what we didn't want. How good are the chances we would get what we wanted?

Not good at all. The same is true when we're putting in our order for Mr. or Ms. Right.

After you have finished reviewing and amending the list, imagine for a moment that you are the person you just wrote about. If you were your Mr./Ms. Right, what would you be looking for in a soul mate?

Since like attracts like, it's very likely that your Mr./Ms. Right is looking for someone who has the same (or complementary) "qualifications" and attributes that you are looking for in them.

Your Self — Improvement List

Now, we come to the final and most crucial part of this exercise. Prepare a second sheet with the same headings. Ask yourself what you need to do to bring yourself up to the same level in each area as your Mr. or Ms. Right. Be sure to write down your answers. It's important to be very honest when doing this.

For example, if you have written on the first sheet under finances that you want them to be debt-free, have a good credit rating and a healthy balance between saving and spending, how do you measure up? Do you have some bills or credit cards to pay off? Do you need to get a better balance between spending and saving?

Whatever tasks or changes you need to make, if any, to bring yourself to the level that you wrote for him/her in the area of finances is what you write on the second sheet under the finances heading.

Do the same thing for each of the headings on the second sheet. Presto! You have created your personal "to do" list for self-improvement.

If you will focus for now on making these improvements to your life, you will become a happier, more complete person. You will attract happy, complete people like you into your life. And, the chances are good that your Mr. or Ms. Right will be among them.

Things to Remember:

1. The work we do on ourselves is the potential we bring to a relationship.[1]

2. No one can keep our good from coming to us.

3. What we become will finally attract all that we want.[2]

---

[1] Stephen and Ondrea Levine, *Embracing the Beloved* (New York, NY: Anchor Books, 1996).

[2] Reynolds, The Magic of Goals

Chapter 9

Carolyn and Joe — A Love Story

The single parent of two sons, Carolyn had been divorced for three years from her second husband when she started the singles class.

The second divorce prompted Carolyn to start working with a counselor to take a hard look at her personal history and the family-of-origin patterns which made personal relationships difficult for her.

After a couple of years of counseling, Carolyn's therapist referred her to what he called "the dating class." Carolyn didn't like the idea. She wasn't interested in finding another husband, thank you very much. The counselor encouraged her to attend anyway. Carolyn resisted. The counselor insisted.

Carolyn later shared the reason for her initial reluctance with me. "I had the idea that you were going to tell us women that we should ask men out on dates. I knew I would never want to do that so I didn't want to hear it. But the first night of class, in response to another student's question, you made the comment that you thought new relationships worked better when the man initiates at least the first three dates. Once, I heard that, I became a willing student."

After Carolyn completed the singles course, she began to participate in social activities with other graduates of my singles course. Of the graduate activities, Carolyn later wrote: "The safe opportunity to practice my newly learned skills was very important. The graduate activities were such an important step for me. Having a social life and being around other single people, learning to make conversations, flirt, and set boundaries were all part of the program — all things that are so very important for helping people build healthy relationships."

Although Carolyn was socially shy, she was a whiz on a computer. A night owl, she found the Internet to be a satisfying nighttime diversion for herself after her sons had gone to bed. While exploring the Internet, Carolyn happened onto the matchmaking sites for singles.

At first Carolyn only read the ads.

Then, she responded to a select few of the ads.

Out of the few, she experienced a synergy with one man in particular.

That man was Joe, a physicist, who worked as a teacher and consultant, and was a published author in his field. Joe had been widowed for about a year after a long marriage. Like Carolyn, Joe had both teenagers and a younger child.

At first, they talked through the matchmaking site. Later, they reserved time and chatted with each other on-line. Eventually, they chatted every night. In those nightly chats, which started at 11:00 p.m., they talked openly and honestly with each other about everything and anything. Both highly intelligent, multi-faceted people, Carolyn and Joe always ran out of time before they ran out of topics.

They talked about current events, their personal lives, their hopes and dreams — often until three o'clock in the morning.

Carolyn and Joe had few in-person dates at first because they were both busy people and lived 50 miles apart. So every date was planned and precious.

They got along well with and were liked by each other's children.

By the time they had dated for six months, they began talking about getting married "someday". Now, two years later, they are married and on their honeymoon.

Lesson #9

Be Grateful for Every Relationship That's Gone Before

You've decided to buy a pair of blue jeans. Let's assume for a moment that you've never owned a pair before. You don't know what size you wear, the right brand for you or the kind of "fit" you're looking for. What do you do?

First, you might talk to some friends and get some information or tips from them. Second, you go to a store that sells jeans. Third, you get a sales person to tell you about jeans and the store's selection of them. From this, you choose the apparent best options. Then, you begin to try on jeans until you find the ones that have the look, the feel and the price tag that's right for you.

The jeans you finally take home are the ones you selected after an extensive process of narrowing your options. In a manner of speaking, when you first entered the store, all of the jeans in the store were potentially the ones you would take home. But, with every pair you tried on, you narrowed your choices until you eventually found the pair that met all of your criteria. That final pair is the one you took home. For a variety of reasons, no other pair of jeans made the cut.

Buying jeans is a lot like the process you go through when you are looking for a life partner. You talk to other people who are successfully partnered to get their tips and suggestions. You network and date to find out the range of your options. Then, you begin narrowing your options until you find just the one right person to take home!

Sometimes during the networking phase of your search for Mr. or Ms. Right, you may get discouraged. In the same way you got tired of trying on pair after pair of blue jeans, you get tired of "trying on" potential life partners. It's easy to see how that happens.

Narrowing Your Options

Every man who said he would call again but didn't, and every woman who said she'd like to see you again, but was always too busy to do so, has done you a favor. They have eliminated themselves as possibilities for a relationship with you. They have helped you narrow your options. The man who promised he'd be there for you and invited you to trust your secrets to him but couldn't handle the truth about your son. The woman who couldn't discipline her young child. The person you spent a glorious weekend with who never calls you again. The man who blames you for everything and can't say he's sorry. The woman who isn't over her "ex" yet. The woman who misrepresents her weight as well as the man who lies about the number of times he's been married. Each and every one of those people has done you a favor, a big favor. They have eliminated themselves from the short list of candidates who have long-term potential for you.

Even though it may not seem like it at the time, when your "Not in my Life" pile or "The Heap" gets bigger, your search gets shorter. "The Heap" is supposed to be big. The bigger it gets, the closer you are to finding the one person you will take home with you and keep for a lifetime.

"There is a time for everything and a season for every activity under heaven."

— *Ecclesiastes 3:1*

Chapter 10

Jim and Amy — Our Love Story

I looked up from my desk one afternoon to see a man with a coffee cup in his hand standing in the hallway outside my office door.

"Is this your office?" he asked.

"Yes," I replied.

"I didn't think anyone rented this office because I've never seen a light on in here before."

"Oh, I guess that's because I was on vacation until today. You're new here, aren't you?"

"Yes, my name is Jim."

"Hi, Jim, my name is Amy."

That is how Jim and I met.

The week before, while I was on vacation, Jim moved into the same executive office suite I had moved into only two months prior. Being highly social and extroverted, I had chosen the office next to the kitchen. I wanted to be where the action was. I wanted to hear people talking with each other in the kitchen and to see them walking past my door. I also hoped that some of them might occasionally wave or stop in to say hello.

Jim says I chose to be near the kitchen so I could check out the single men and grab them before they got away.

Jim and I chit-chatted for two or three minutes that first day, and the next day, and the next day. Sometimes, Jim stopped by twice in one day and other days not at all. He always stood in the doorway while we talked, not wanting to interrupt my work. When the phone rang, he would say good-bye and leave.

One afternoon about two weeks later, I convinced Jim to come in and sit down — "just until the phone rings." We had a nice conversation in which I learned some things about him personally — what a good father and friend he is to his young adult sons and how proud he is of both of them. He keeps in frequent contact with them through phone calls, E-mail and visits.

That afternoon, the phone didn't ring for 40 minutes!

Jim says I tricked him. He says I unplugged the phone and "lured" him into my office.

I must admit that when I first found out that Jim was single and new in town, I shamelessly recruited him for my singles class. First, I gave him the brochure and schedule. Then I followed up with him four times until he agreed to sign up for the course. Jim told me he didn't need a singles course. "I'm not looking," he said. "If it happens, it happens." Fateful words.

To hear Jim tell it, he started the singles course with one arm twisted behind his back and one eye on the teacher.

Since Jim and I were office neighbors who talked to each other daily, I considered him first a friend and secondly a student.

One afternoon, Jim asked if I would help him pick out a pair of frames for his new glasses. (What woman could resist an invitation like that?)

I spent 40 minutes helping him pick out the new frames after work one afternoon. The next morning, he thanked me for the favor and told me he would like to buy me dinner as a thank-you. Although I thought he was being very generous, I accepted.

It was two months later when we went out for that dinner. By that time, the dinner was officially a "date", our first.

We went to an Italian restaurant on the coldest November day since the Ice Age. I was chilled to the bone. As I clutched a mug of hot coffee for the warmth, Jim sipped a glass of red wine. After about fifteen minutes, he moved his hand and knocked over his glass of dark red wine. In an attempt to grab the wine glass, he knocked over his large tumbler of ice water, too. A deep pink river of wine and water ran across the white tablecloth, dropped onto the vacant chair on the other side of the table, and splashed, finally, onto the floor.

The waiter quickly and graciously cleared the table, mopped the floor, and replaced everything, including the glass of wine.

Then, when we'd had a chance to catch our breaths, Jim leaned over and whispered to me, "I guess that's what I get for groping." "What?" I asked. He repeated, "I guess that's what I get for groping...I was reaching to take your hand. I was going to touch it to see if you had warmed up any, but I really just wanted to hold your hand."

Women reading this are all thinking, "Oh, how romantic." The men can take a lesson from Jim.

What was so touching about this scene was that Jim self-disclosed his thoughts and positive intent even when he didn't have to. That was the trait he had that I was surprised and touched by again and again as we dated. He would tell me what he was thinking about himself, me, our relationship. I felt so cherished when he told me about those things.

Jim and I talked easily, and we talked a lot. We talked about things of substance and things of silliness. Old stuff, new stuff, most any stuff. What we did not talk about was marriage. Being persuasive by nature, I stayed away from that subject. I wanted to be sure that when Jim asked me to marry him it was truly his idea, free of pressure from me. I privately vowed not to say the "M-word" until he first broached the subject. I decided to wait him out until he was ready. It was a long wait.

Although we didn't talk about marriage, I was never in doubt about Jim's love for me or his commitment to me and our relationship. Those things were made clear by his day-to-day words and actions.

By the time we had dated for several months, we each knew that we had found the right person and that we would get married. There were a number of times I expected (and hoped) that Jim might pop the question: Our one-year anniversary, the cruise we took three months later, holidays, Valentine's Day, our second anniversary. Nothing.

I am a planner. Jim is a let-it-happen kind of guy. Here's how the proposal happened.

We spent a beautiful Sunday afternoon visiting model homes, something that we enjoyed doing from time to time. The idea was to find a house that Jim might like to buy "someday". Well, that Sunday we found a model home for sale that both Jim and I loved the minute we walked in.

Back at my apartment that evening, Jim chatted on and on about the house. Did I really like it? He really liked it. He wanted to buy it. Did I want to buy it with him? I responded by asking him how that would fit with his previous statements that he would never live with anyone unless he was married. Silence. Change of subject.

Twenty minutes later, Jim proposed.

We got engaged, bought the house, moved in and got married several months later —— very close to our third anniversary.

Some time later, Jim shared that he had considered the cruise an opportunity to get married. Although I would have welcomed getting married then, I'm glad we didn't. The way things turned, out we had an additional year and a half to get to know each other better. We got to enjoy dating and being "numero uno" with each other longer without the distractions and pressures of planning a wedding and setting up and maintaining a blended household.

Jim and I took our time building our relationship step-by-step. And, yes, we adhered to the 300-hour rule. We were definitely best friends and intimates before we were lovers. We also maintained a good bit of autonomy while we were dating.

We didn't fall into the trap of "playing house." We had separate apartments 15 minutes apart from each other. We had a date for dinner every Wednesday night and spent most of each weekend together. Other than Jim's bicycle, which stayed at my place for spontaneous bike rides on weekend mornings, Jim took all of his personal belongings home with him every time he left.

As married people, we each have one room and a bathroom that we don't share, and we still reserve Wednesday nights and weekends for each other.

We were married in a simple ceremony with family, close friends and 50 graduates of the singles course in attendance. We honeymooned in Maui, my "dream" destination.

It took Jim and me 10 years to find each other, but well worth the wait.

Lesson #10

Mr./Ms. Right is Looking for You, Too

As you search for your soul mate, it is important to remember that you are not alone. Mr. or Ms. Right is looking for you and is wanting to find you as much as you want to find him or her.

No one knows for sure how any of us will meet our future mate. Sometimes we think we do know, and sometimes we think it should happen a certain way and at a certain time, preferably NOW.

However, as much as we don't like the idea of not having control of when, where and how we meet our mate, it is not up to us when it happens. As Jim says, "When it happens, it happens."

"So what am I supposed to do between now and then?" you ask.

Preparing for Mr./Ms. Right

First, you need to get your life working for you. You need to get personal business, both internal and external, squared away. I don't mean that everything has to be perfect, but you do need to have things in your life under control and moving in the direction of improvement or completion. You need to be living a balanced life.

Next, you have to create the kind of lifestyle for yourself that you would like to have with a partner.

Finally, you need to get yourself into the mainstream socially. To accomplish this, go where you are drawn to go. Try things that appeal to you. Invite other people into your life. Volunteer with organizations whose goals match up with your highest values.

The most common way to meet one's mate is to be introduced by a mutual friend. The second most common way to meet is when you are both involved in an activity that you like to do — one that is a significant part of your life, something that you do again and again because you derive pleasure from doing so.

Getting Out and Networking

Networking is a necessary and invaluable tool for single people. You need to develop networking skills. Networking means getting yourself out of your cave and around other people.

Networking activities range from intense outings like singles mixers to topic-focused activities, or classes, to the relatively solitary act of plopping yourself down with the morning paper at a bagel shop or breakfast cafe.

All of these activities include being around other people, but there is a big difference in the number of people with whom you are likely to interact. The bigger the number, the greater the intensity.

The level of intensity you choose may sometimes reflect your personality. Extraverts, people who are charged up by contact with other people, are generally attracted to larger groups and to events where direct contact with others is expected. Introverts, because they take a while to feel comfortable around people they don't already know, tend to prefer smaller groups and activities that meet on a recurring basis.

There will be times when your energy level will drive your decision. The best time to propel yourself out the door is when you are feeling good. That is when you have the energy to handle the stress of a new situation and new people.

On the other hand, when you are feeling out of sorts, it is probably a good idea to spend time alone or with a trusted friend. Forcing yourself to be social now will probably not work and may make it harder for you to venture forth in the future.

It helps to go to mixers and parties with someone you know and like. That way, you can introduce your friend to people you know, and he or she can return the favor. Chances are your friend's friends are people you will also like — definitely a win-win situation.

Another benefit of "tag-team" networking is that each of you has the opportunity to brag about your friend which is something they cannot do themselves.

Here are some additional tips taken from Susan Roan's book, "How to Work a Room". Susan suggests that we adopt "host behavior" when we go to a party. By this, she means that instead of being passive, like a guest, we should be active, like a host.

Susan goes on to explain that if this were your party, you would be greeting people at the door with a hello and a handshake. You would be taking their coats or directing them to where the coats are being collected. You would be answering inquiries about the location of restrooms and you would be showing people where the food was and offering to get them something to drink. You would also be introducing the newcomers to guests already there. Throughout all of this, you would be wearing a smile.

The next time you are invited to a party or other social gathering, try out some of this host behavior. Your host or hostess will be grateful; the other guests will be grateful; you will feel useful; other guests will view you as a friend and are likely to seek you out for conversation. And, isn't that what you came for?

This "trick" is especially good for introverts as it gives them a role within which to operate, allows them to meet people one at a time and puts them in charge of the interaction. What could be better? Try it!

Another networking strategy is to challenge yourself to meet everyone in the room. My student, Rita, an introvert, did this the first time she attended one of the singles course dinners. She just stuck out her hand to the first person she saw and introduced herself. She then moved on around the room, table by table, until she had met everyone. Her overtures were well received by others, and she felt happy and proud of herself.

From personal experience, I can tell you that you have to start from the moment you enter the room. If you wait until you get comfortable, you will chicken out.

One more tip — take business cards with you to give to people you would like to stay in touch with. Write your home phone number on your card if you prefer they call you there.

Networking includes anything and everything you might do to meet people. Networking does not, however, include sitting beside the phone hoping it will ring. Pick up the phone and call someone.

That's what hands are for!

Chapter 11

Tying it All Together

A number of common themes run through the stories of these ten couples.

Individually, they made conscious decisions to change their lives for the better. Anna stated it most clearly, but everyone who attended the singles class made a commitment to themselves for positive change.

Individually, they took some time to get their lives in balance. In some cases, the time was as short as a year or two while, for Barb, it was a decade.

Individually, they were open to learning new information. Both counseling and classes were frequently mentioned.

Individually, they had values and goals that shaped their lives. Remember Becky's goal to own a brick home with blueberry bushes and flower gardens?

Individually, they had hobbies and interests that gave them pleasure. Debbie played cards, Carolyn surfed the Internet, Becky and Katie loved dancing.

Individually, they were clear about who they were and whom they were looking for. Barb wanted to be wanted, not needed.

Individually, they were willing to accept invitations and to meet new people. Katie, for instance went to a singles dance with her classmates and met Carl — her Mr. Right.

Individually, they maintained their standards even when it meant they would have to wait longer. Becky vowed to be celibate until she found Mr. Right. "If it takes forever to find him, then so be it."

Individually, they viewed marriage as serious and permanent.

As a couple, they spent a lot of time together just talking with each other. Susi and Ron spent "hours and hours" talking. Debbie and Randy, Becky and John spent many hours playing cards together and talking. Carolyn and Joe chatted on-line for hours every night.

As a couple, they took their time getting to know each other before getting married. Not one of these couples rushed into marriage during the early period of infatuation. Some postponed becoming sexually intimate until they were truly best friends and intimates, and others waited until they were married.

The couples met in a variety of ways. Three couples, Bart and Tina, Barb and John, Jim and Amy, met at work. Mutual friends introduced Mike to Lisa. Two couples, Susi and Ron, Anna and Dan, had known each other earlier in their lives. Carolyn and Joe met through a matchmaking service on-line while Debbie and

Randy met while playing cards on-line. Becky and John, like Katie and Carl met at singles dances.

Those previously married considered their new partnership the gift of a second chance.

My experience as The Singles Coach has taught me that it is not possible to predict when, where or how a couple will meet. They meet when, where and how it happens. The many personal decisions each party makes prior to their meeting, however, seem to be instrumental in their being in the right place at the right time. Remember Amy's decision to rent the office next to the kitchen?

I have come to believe that Cupid loves tricks and surprises. So many times, the person in the package we're looking for is a disappointment while the person in the easily over-looked package turns out to be our soul mate. Often, our soul mate is the one who challenges us to grow in an area we would prefer to ignore. It's not unusual that we first have to overcome a deep fear or change an erroneous but deeply held belief about ourselves in order to be ready to meet our soul mate.

Cupid also surprises us in ways we really like, such as when Mr. or Ms. Right turns out be more than we expected and treats us better than we hoped for. Sometimes the surprise is that we get to feel a deeper happiness and contentment in our lives than we ever dreamed possible.

If it hasn't happened for you yet, take heart, it will happen for you.

It doesn't matter what your personal history has been or what your perceived deficits are. When you get your life in balance and working for you, you become an irresistibly desirable person — a perfect match for your soul mate.

Mr. or Ms. Right is looking for you right now.

Believe it!

Suggested Reading

Chapman, Dr. Gary. *The Five Love Languages*. Chicago, IL: Northfield Publishing, 1992.

Cloud, Henry and Townsend, John. *Boundaries*. Scranton, PA: Harper Mass Market Paperbacks, 1996.

De Angelis, Dr. Barbara. *The Real Rules*. New York, NY: Dell Publishing, 1997.

Gray, Dr. John. *Men Are from Mars, Women Are from Venus*. New York, NY: HarperCollins Publishers, Inc., 1992.

_____. *Mars and Venus Together Forever*. New York, NY: HarperCollins Publishers, Inc., 1994.

_____. *Mars and Venus In the Bedroom*. New York, NY: HarperCollins Publishers, Inc., 1995.

_____. *Mars and Venus On A Date*. New York, NY: HarperCollins Publishers, Inc., 1997.

_____. *Mars and Venus Starting Over*. New York, NY: HarperCollins Publishers, Inc., 1998.

Page, Susan. *If I Am So Wonderful, Why Am I Still Single?* New York, NY: Viking Penguin Group, Inc., 1988.

_____. *The Eight Essential Traits of Couples Who Thrive*. Westminster, MD: Bantam Doubleday Dell, 1977.

_____. *How One of You Can Bring the Two of You Together*. Westminster, MD: Bantam Doubleday Dell, 1998.

Walker, Pam. *How To Find Mr. Right*. Dayton, OH: Agape Publications, 1993.

Wegscheider-Cruse, Sharon. *Learning to Love Yourself*. Deerfield Beach, FL: Health Communications, Inc., 1987.

About the Author

Amy M. Owens, The Singles Coach, is a marriage counselor in private practice in Indianapolis whose specialty is coaching singles who are serious about finding life partners. With a Master's Degree in Counseling and 25 years experience in the human relations field as a counselor, group leader, author, workshop leader, professional speaker and teacher, Amy brings to the classroom a rich blend of professional training and personal experience.

Divorced and "single" for 10 years following a 24-year marriage, Amy remarried a year ago. In 1995, Amy created an educational program for adult singles to help them get ready "from the inside out" to attract their Mr. or Ms. Right into their lives. That program, Advanced Relationship Strategies for Singles (ARS), has positively impacted the personal lives of the hundreds of students who have participated in it.

The ARS program provides a stimulating but safe forum in which adult singles of any age can learn and practice effective dating and relationship development skills. Students who complete the program graduate confident that they can attract, meet, and date desirable people, and that they can create healthy, satisfying, enduring love relationships. They believe they can, and will, find their Mr. or Ms. Right.

In *Take Heart!*, The Singles Coach lovingly shares the stories of ten of her students who married. Each story is paired with a lesson that the couple had to learn on the way to the altar. Some of the Ten Lessons are taken directly from the ARS course.

Amy Owens is the founder and co-sponsor with St. Luke's Singles of the Midwest Singles Weekend, one of the largest networking and educational forums in the U.S. The Singles Weekend is held annually in February in Indianapolis.

More information about the ARS program and the Midwest Singles Weekend is available on Amy's Web site:

www.thesinglescoach.com.

To contact Amy about speaking engagements, please write or call:
www.info@thesinglescoach.com or **1-317-805-4950.**

For Additional Books:

Ordered by:

Name_____

Address_____

City_____ State_____

Zip_____

Email address:_____

Day Phone (   )_____

Eve. Phone (   )_____

☐ MasterCard   ☐ Visa   ☐ American Express Acct.

Card #_____

Expiration Date: _____

Signature: _____

Make checks/money orders payable to: **Connections**

Items Ordered

Qty	Title	Unit Price	Total
	Take Heart!	$9.95	

	Shipping & Handling	$2.00	
IN Residents add 5% tax per book $ .50			
	Total of order		$_____

Connections Publishing
9465 Counselors Row, Suite 200
Indianapolis, IN 46240

www.info@thesinglescoach.com
1-317-805-4950

☐ I would like information about *Take Heart!* lectures and
workshops by Amy Owens.

Thank You for Your Order!